# Principals of Culture Bible
# First Nations of Australia

**TRISH FRAIL**

Ordering Information:

Prime Seven Media
518 Landmann St.
Tomah City, WI 54660

Printed in the United States of America

# Introduction

With the First Nations people being the oldest surviving culture in the world yet parts of the Spirituality belief of the First Nations has been slowly forgotten as time has passed by.

This booklet is to help the Spiritual belief live.

All tribes/clans have different language, for this booklet the word Creator is used to describe the Spirits who created the world and the lore's. You can use the name that your tribe/clan has always used for the Creator.

Over the years some of the First Nations people have lost or have been denied various principals and lore's of their culture.

The Spirituality of the First Nations people does not have one single spirit that they believe in, rather it is divided into separate roles;

The Creator who created the people, the land and the environment.

Ancestral Beings who showed the First Nations people how to live on the land and in the environment, they laid down lore's and ceremonies for the people to follow, this was during the period of the Dreaming.

Both have always been acknowledged in ceremonies. Some tribes/clans have more spirits who contributed in the creating of their people and the land.

It is acknowledged that some tribes and clans have different lore's, however there are a few principals of First Nations people that are the same regardless where you are in Australia. It is also acknowledged that not all tribes/clans will have the following lore's.

The First Nations belief in Spirituality and European Religion can and do co-exist. If you believe in another religion, then continue to do so, but acknowledge your spirituality and the spirituality of your tribe/clan.

It is also acknowledged that there are a lot of different cultures and religions within Australia and together by respecting each other including respecting our different spirituality beliefs we can all live in harmony.

The people of the First Nations can visit anywhere within Australia and there are some main lore's that all tribes / clans follow, in this bible we have gathered some of the main lore's of the First Nations culture.

Please note: The spirituality Corroboree grounds is a way of describing where you go after life.

**Suggested First Nations Prayer for the Creator**

**Ohh Creator**

**My Creator,**

**I have been inspired by you,**

**And the other Spirits of this land**

**The land of the Dreaming**

**I thank thee**

**For all that you have done for me,**

**my family and my community**

**For the tree of life leads us down many roads**

**Help me down those roads**

**Help me with our Culture**

**Our Ways**

**The Ways of the Creator**

**Thank You**

*Standard guitar tuning for the National Anthem* (4/4 tempo)

The Life of Thee

D
*The rhythm of the feet, pounding on the earth*

   C              G
*My creator, oh how I love thee*

D
*The clapsticks keep in tune*

*Come, come sing with me*

C         G
*Ohhhhh how I love thee*

D
*The spirits watching over me as my feet pound the earth,*

C
*Walking or dancing as I enjoy my life*

        G
*Ohhhhh how I love thee*

**(BRIDGE)**

Em                    G
*Corroboree, corroboree as we come together,*

   C           G
*For together we are one*

Em            G
*The tribal lands are forever in my heart,*

     C
*As my feet pound the earth*

        D
*Ohhhhh how I love thee*

D
*My culture, my land, my family, my spirits*

   C        G
*My creator, how I love thee*

# Dreamtime / Dreaming

*D*reaming is a time when the earth and the universe were being created

When the spirits came down to earth and made the animals, rivers, mountains, plants and trees humans and all things on earth.

The spirits set down the lore's and laws for all to follow, we cannot change those.

The Dreaming belongs to all First Nations people

The Dreaming is the spirituality of the First Nations people

The stories that relate to the Dreaming pass on the values of life, lore's, laws through storytelling, dance, songs and paintings.

The links to the Dreaming are life, culture and lore, initiations, sacred sites and ceremonies.

The ancestor spirits did not leave the earth when their work was done, but remained on earth thus linking the past, present and future to the people of the land

The First Nations people understand where they belong and their connection to spirituality through the Dreaming.

Please note:

The term Dreaming or Dreamtime is not a traditional word, however it is a word that is now commonly used as other cultures do not understand the concept or religion of the beginning of life or the spirituality of the First Nations people.

The Torres Strait Islander people did not have a Dreaming their spirituality is related to stories of Tagai, which identify the Torres Strait Islanders as sea people.

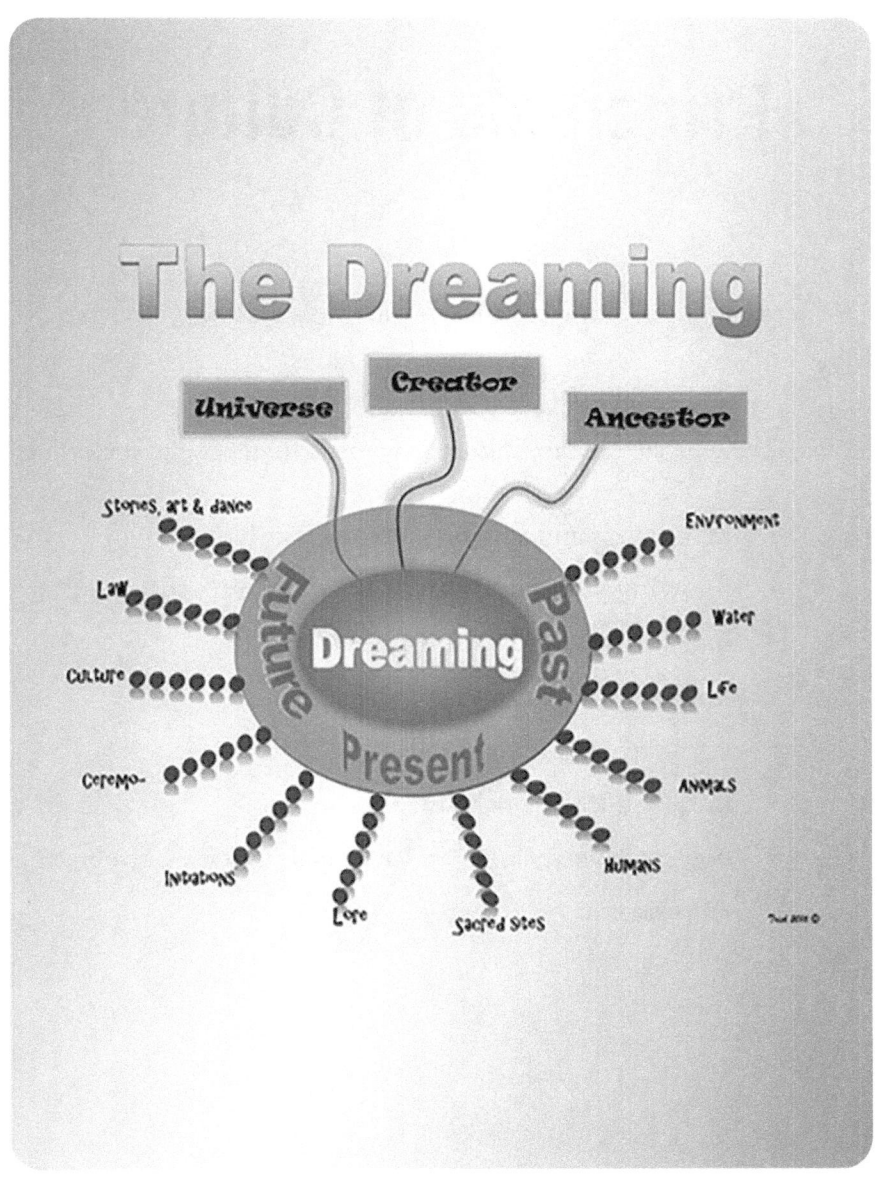

# Principals of Culture

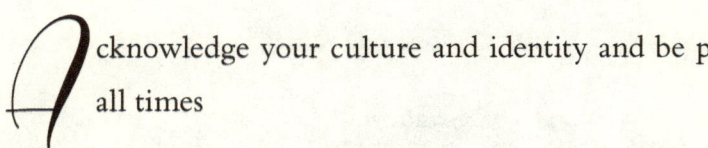cknowledge your culture and identity and be proud of it at all times

- To be proud of your culture may mean many things including,

    - ✓ being with and supporting your family
    - ✓ knowing your family and how all are related
    - ✓ knowing your tribe's/clan's history
    - ✓ knowing language
    - ✓ knowing traditional foods
    - ✓ knowing traditional dance and music
    - ✓ being active in local and national activities celebrating cultural etc.

# Totems

ost tribes/clans ban those from hunting and eating the totems that relate to them, whilst some make exceptions for special occasions, if you are unsure check with your Elders.

Know your tribe/clan Totem

- Ask your Elders, if your Elders are unsure, ask them if they know someone who might know or contact the local Aboriginal Land Council or local First Nations organisations. Know your families Totem

- Ask your Elders, again if your Elders are unsure, ask them if they know someone who might know. Know your personal Totem

- If you were not given a personal Totem, ask the Spirits for one. At times we are given nicknames that reflect our personality, this might be your totem or meditate and seek your totem, it may not come straight away, keep mediating, hopefully the spirits will grant you your totem.

All family Totems are passed through from the mothers side,

- Women carry the genes of family, and look after the kinship of the family thus women carry the family totems

When children are born, you must wait for their personality to emerge (about 12months) before giving them their Totem.

- A totem might relate to what the mother or father were doing or where they were when the mother went into labour or the totem might relate to the child's personality

Before you pass over if you can, call for the Spirits of your Totems

- You will have the opportunity to ask them to show you the way to the Spiritual Corroboree grounds.

Respect all sacred land and objects

- Seek approval and only if you have approval from the tribe/clan who are in charge of the sacred land and objects can you go on the sacred land or touch the sacred objects.

When entering on to another tribe/clan land you must acknowledge that you are on their land.

- If possible introduce yourself to an Elder or a member from that land, if that is not possible than say words to the effect, your name and what tribe you are from and that you acknowledge that you are on their land, will respect their land, and do not plan to do any wrong.

No copulating with children (having sex)

- It is the responsibility of all to look after and protect children. Under various tribe/clans in traditional times, if you had sexual relations with children you would be put to death an example was to be tied down on a bull-ant nest and left to die.

No copulating with family members of the same family totem

- Family members have the same genetic makeup and if the genes are too closely connected it will cause sickness in the genes of the children. Some tribes/clans the brother and sisters are not allowed to speak to each other when they become 'teenagers' to prevent them from copulating with each other. Please note, the kinship of family includes brothers, sisters, cousins and friends who have been brought up closely.

Learn your tribes/clans Dreaming stories, for you are the custodian of the story

- If no family members know your tribes Dreaming stories, research and ask other Elders, the Land Councils, other local First Nations organisations, local libraries etc.

Pass your Dreaming stories on to the younger generation members of your family's totems and the tribes/clans totem

- Although the First Nations history is an oral history we are now in a different era, for our culture to survive we need to write down Dreamtime history and family stories thus preventing them from becoming lost. If need be, seek assistance to write down your stories.

After there has been a death, have a smoking ceremony

- A smoking ceremony allows the spirits to go free to the Spiritual Corroboree grounds.
- The smoking takes away the bad spirits while cleansing and healing all as you walk through it.

# Regardless of where you live there are lore's that you should follow

Such as;

- Show Elders respect
- Children are to be respected and cared for at all times
- Respect and care for the land as the land is of the Dreaming
- Care for the animals of the land
- Care for the environment

Please name a few of your personal /tribe lore's that you follow

# Welcome to Country or Acknowledgement of Country

*D*uring traditional times, when entering another tribes land, you had to wait at various locations to be invited on to the land and you would be Welcome to the Country (in other societies you would knock on someone's door and wait to be invited in). Not being invited in, is what we would now call trespassing and it would cause fictions between tribes/clans.

In today's way of life, we still do Welcome to Country or Acknowledgement of Country however we don't seek permission to cross into different nations these days as we would have had to in the days of Aboriginal nations boundaries.

We should always acknowledge the people of that nation that we are visiting or currently residing in, as they are the custodians of that nation.

Always get to know the local traditional community.

If you are from the land you can do Welcome to Country, however if you are not from that land you must do Acknowledgement of Country

Always seek a local Elderly person who is well respected within the community to do Welcome to Country or Acknowledgement of Country. This is part of an opening ceremony perforable the first item, with a smoking ceremony if possible.

All people can do Acknowledgement of Country.

If you have been asked to do Welcome to Country or Acknowledgement of Country

Introduce yourself with your name and your tribe/clan (if you are Aboriginal or Torres Strait Islander)

If you are doing Acknowledgment of Country, you must state that you are doing Acknowledgement of Country

Acknowledge the tribal land of which you stand on

Pay your respects to the traditional custodians of the land of which you are standing upon

Pay your respect to the Elders both past and present

Acknowledge the ceremony of which you are part off

Welcome all to the Country (if you are a traditional custodian of the land) and hope that they will enjoy the ceremony

If you are doing Acknowledgement of Country, hope that they will enjoy the ceremony.

## Language is important this may help you with your language

| Traditional word | What does the word mean | What tribe is the word from |
|---|---|---|
|  |  |  |
|  |  |  |
|  |  |  |
|  |  |  |
|  |  |  |
|  |  |  |
|  |  |  |
|  |  |  |
|  |  |  |
|  |  |  |
|  |  |  |
|  |  |  |
|  |  |  |
|  |  |  |
|  |  |  |
|  |  |  |
|  |  |  |
|  |  |  |
|  |  |  |
|  |  |  |
|  |  |  |
|  |  |  |
|  |  |  |
|  |  |  |
|  |  |  |
|  |  |  |
|  |  |  |
|  |  |  |
|  |  |  |
|  |  |  |
|  |  |  |

**Please write a Dreamtime Story of your Tribe/Clan (you can seek assistance to write your Dreamtime Story).**

**Please write a Family Story that an Elder told you**

Draw a tribal map of your tribal land and name all of the tribes connected to your tribe/clan boundaries.

# Tindale Map

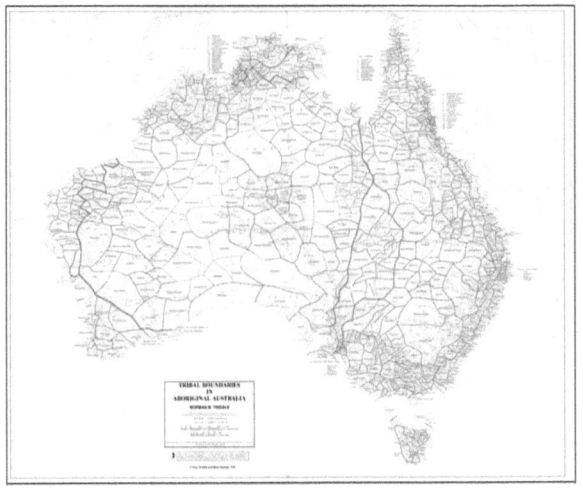

Disclaimer

This map is a reproduction of N.B. Tindale's 1974 map of Indigenous group boundaries existing at the time of first European settlement in Australia. It is not intended to represent contemporary relationships to the land.

©Tony Tindale and Beryl George, 1974. Courtesy of the South Australian Museum.

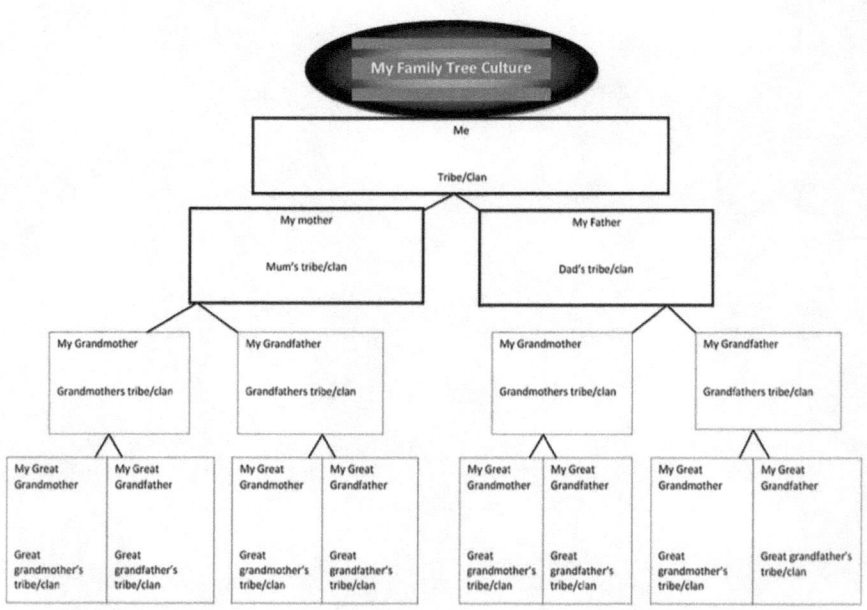

**This page is for additional information for your family tree**

Partner:

Tribal /Clan Totem:

Children

Siblings

Nieces

Nephews

Aunties

Uncles

Great Aunties

Great Uncles

Cousins

## Personal details of the owner of this booklet

Name:

DOB:

Tribe/Clan:

Tribe/Clan Totem:

Family Totem:

Personal Totem:

# Biography

*T*rish is a Ngemba woman from Brewarrina, western NSW with 4 sisters and 1 brother.

She left school when she was 14, her mother died when she was 15 and she became pregnant at 16.

Trish has five wonderful children, 4 daughters Mary, Jelina, Cherrie, Charlee-Sue and 1 son Alex and 4 gorgeous grandchildren and many more who call her Nanna Trish, she overcame a lot of life's challenges with no formal education yet she still secured senior Management positions and worked tirelessly for communities.

Trish's partner Barry and his son Sean asked Trish to explain more of the First Nationals culture to them, after a lot of research she realised that a book explaining some of the lore's of the culture needed to be written.

As soon as Trish commenced writing the words flowed.

Trish hopes this booklet will help people and give them some structural guidelines of the First Nations culture.

Trish would like to thank all those who helped and advised her with the writing of this book especially her children and partner who encouraged her also her nanna May and Aunty Betty who told her a lot of the Ngemba history and the First Nations Culture.

Trish would also like to thank her daughter Mary for the art work of the three spirits and her son-in-law Mike Green who wrote the music for the anthem 'The life of thee' and all of her children for the editing.

The oldest manmade structure in the world is on the land of the Ngemba people, the Ngunnhu Guya (Fish Traps) at Brewarrina made by our Creator, Biami and his two sons, Booma-ooma-nowi and Ghinda-inda-mui (both words are from the Ualar language) tribes from around the area would come and fish, they were always welcomed for sharing ceremonies, lore and law, marriage and to resolve conflict. Biami placed the Ngemba people as the custodians of the Ngunnhu.

Trish can be contacted at kooriways@gmail.com

www.ingramcontent.com/pod-product-compliance
Lightning Source LLC
Chambersburg PA
CBHW031242120626
46545CB00003B/1236